101 HAMMOND B3 TIPS

STUFF ALL THE PROS KNOW AND USE

BY BRIAN CHARETTE

PLAYBACK+
Speed • Pitch • Balance • Loop

To access audio visit:
www.halleonard.com/mylibrary

1566-0548-0898-2421

T0057618

ISBN 978-1-4803-9370-7

Copyright © 2014 by HAL LEONARD CORPORATION
International Copyright Secured All Rights Reserved

Visit Hal Leonard Online at
www.halleonard.com

Contact us:
Hal Leonard
7777 West Bluemound Road
Milwaukee, WI 53213
Email: info@halleonard.com

In Europe, contact:
Hal Leonard Europe Limited
42 Wigmore Street
Marylebone, London, W1U 2RN
Email: info@halleonardeurope.com

In Australia, contact:
Hal Leonard Australia Pty. Ltd.
4 Lentara Court
Cheltenham, Victoria, 3192 Australia
Email: info@halleonard.com.au

TABLE OF CONTENTS

Tip		Page

INTRODUCTION

This book you hold in your hands is a guide to the most important concepts for playing the Hammond B3 organ. Let's start with just a few notes about the examples, then we can dive in. When speaking about drawbar settings, we will use a nomenclature of nine numbers that go from 0–8, suggesting how far each of the corresponding drawbars should be pulled out. For example, 458000008 would mean the first drawbar to the left of the set would be pulled out to 4, the second bar to 5, the third to 8, bars 4–8 pushed all the way in, the last bar pulled all the way out. Notes will also be given on vibrato, percussion, and Leslie speaker settings. Unless notated, the lower manual will be set to 808000000 – or 838000000 for walking a bass line. The pedals will be set to 70. Vibrato settings unless otherwise specified should be set to C3.

Many of the examples will be given with walking bass lines. If you are playing mostly with a bassist, comp on the lower manual with a setting that has the first two drawbars pushed all the way in. This enables you to play comping chords on the lower manual in the way a pianist would accompany his own solo. Use a setting like 005780000 or 008800000 for the lower manual. I suggest you try the examples with the bass, though, because I believe that playing the lower manual and pedals is essential for B3 mastery. The pedal stave on the music sounds an octave lower; that should be understood for all examples. For easy reading, the second space on the bass staff will correspond to the C in the middle of the pedals. The music examples are quite simple and are meant to be transposed into 12 keys once mastered.

THE JIMMY SMITH SETTING

Hailing from Norristown, Pennsylvania, Jimmy Smith was a pianist who switched to organ full time after hearing "Wild Bill" Davis. Smith is unquestionably the most influential Hammond organist and is widely regarded as the instrument's top player. His percussive bebop solos and left-hand walking bass, with pedal pumping, codified the sound of jazz organ. The example below shows the most common top manual drawbar setting Smith used to spin his bluesy riffs. This setting is also referred to as "all tabs up" because the percussion tabs all select the top switches: on/soft/fast/3rd harmonic. The notes from this Smith-inspired blues come from the G blues scale (G-Bb-C-C#-D-F-G). The crunch of blue notes sounding together with screaming trills and shakes are the hallmarks of this style of playing. In bar 3, a triplet phrase connects our shakes and dissonant lines. Notice also the bass pedal technique. Pump lightly with a flat foot on the B in the middle of the pedal staff and occasionally walk a line with heel-to-toe motion for chromatic scales. The B is a resonant note and the occasional pedal walking provides interesting motion to the bass line. When you tap, touch the pedals lightly and with a short sustain to get just the thump of the attack without the pitch fully developing. Set your pedal drawbars to 71.

 TIP 1

888000000   on/soft/fast/3rd   C3 Vib/Leslie Brake

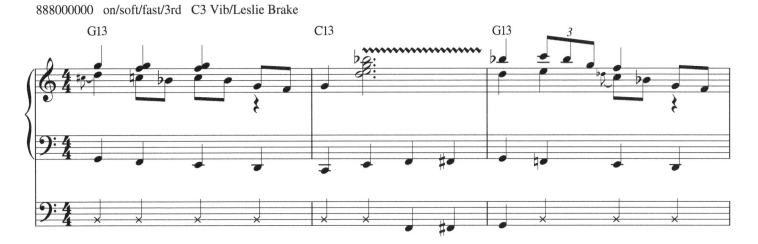

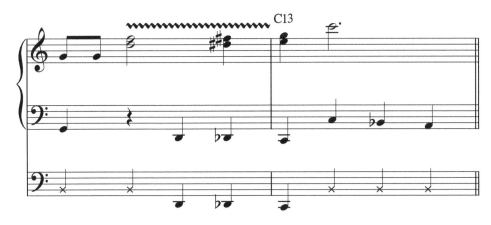

THE HALF-FAT SETTING

This is an effective setting to emulate big band backgrounds behind a horn solo. The setting is called "half-fat" because it's somewhere between all the stops out and the more chill comping settings. Our voicings are four-note 6th and 7th shapes coming from the C Mixolydian mode (C-D-E-F-G-A-B♭-C) with chromatic embellishments à la Count Basie. The bass line is a simple blues ostinato with the pedals just pumping the B. When you gliss off the C6 chord at the end of bar 1, try to smear the whole fleshy part of your hand over the black and white keys. With the Leslie set to fast, this is very effective. Use the volume pedal to stab the chord quickly, then gently ride back.

This pedal technique works in tandem with the pumping bass to give the organ its swampy groove. Make sure not to overdo it with the volume pedal, though. Many beginning organists rock in time with the pedal, a dead giveaway that they're a little green to Organland. Try to be relaxed in all your limbs as you play, because it takes a lot of energy to play organ. There's a subtle feeling that you will experience after playing organ for a while, when the pedals, volume, solo, comping, and settings are working together to make one sound. This is a big "Aha!" moment that will give you a real feeling of the greasy bounce you need to be a real Hammond organist.

 TIP 2

888000888   perc off   C3 Vib/Leslie fast

Mel Rhyne came to prominence playing with Wes Montgomery as part of his dynamic organ trio. Rhyne's sound was a lot different than Smith's. Three of the first four drawbars are out and the second harmonic is used in the percussion. The volume of the percussion is set to normal, which gives a little more click. The decay is also different. A slow decay means that the sound of the percussion dies away more slowly, creating a more legato sound. In this example, inspired by Mel, we use a B♭ major scale and descending F7 dominant bebop scale (F-E-E♭-D-C-B♭-A-G-F) with a few chromatic embellishments. The lines usually change direction quickly, often with an arpeggiated leap preceding a scalar descent with chromatic embellishments. The D♭ in the right hand at the end of bar 1 is a chromatic note leading to the strong downbeat of bar 2's Cmin7 chord.

The trick with bebop lines is to combine the chromatics and scales to make phrases that resolve over the bar line. This is the secret to swinging; it's not just about accenting every other eighth note. Notice how the Ddim arpeggio outlines the G7♭9 harmony in bar 3 and how a Bmaj7 arpeggio works as a tritone substitution in bar 4. Be on the lookout for simple root-position arpeggios and shapes that, when played over different bass notes, make interesting harmonies. On your next gig, when you see a 7♭9 chord, think of the dim7th chord a 5th above the root to supply a soloing or comping idea. The pedals just thump on the B.

 TIP 3

884800000   on/norm/slow/2nd   No Vib/Leslie

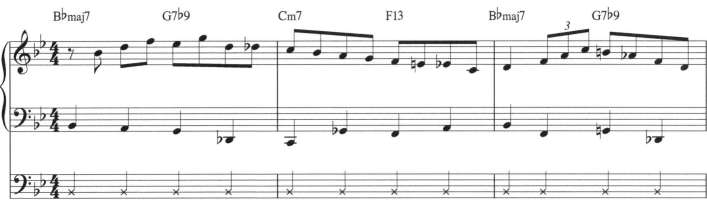

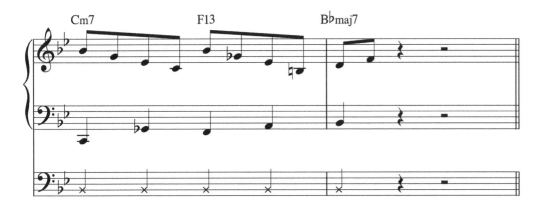

A lot of people don't know it, but pianist Erroll Garner was one of the first Hammond organists. This is the setting most attributed to him. The percussion tabs are set like Jimmy Smith's, but the drawbars are different; pull the first and last four all the way out and put the Leslie to fast. The most common way to use this setting is to play octaves with the thumb and fifth finger of the right hand. The middle fingers smash the notes in between, creating the illusion that real chords are being played. Gently rock your hand back and forth while doing this also. The middle fingers can be curled under or left flat. The key to this technique is all in the wrist. Experiment rocking your wrist back and forth so that the top and bottom notes of the "chord" shake loosely back and forth at slightly different times. The volume pedal should be almost all the way back with just little stabs for emphasis, then right back to grooving.

Squabbling, as this technique is often called, works particularly well in keys like C and E♭, the key of the example below. The bass line is a simple root-fifth walking ballad with the pedals pumping. Try going heel-to-toe for the two walk-downs, then back to pumping. The notes in the right hand come mostly from the E♭ major pentatonic scale (E♭-F-G-B♭-C-E♭). Notice how much mileage we get with this simple scale over the whole four-bar progression. Remember to rock your hand gently and quickly back and forth and try to smash the middle notes as much as possible.

 TIP 4

800008888   on/soft/fast/3rd   C3 Vib/Leslie fast

THE GROOVE HOLMES SETTING

Richard "Groove" Holmes was rumored to step on a bunch of pedals at once to add beef to his killer bass lines. Many say he was the main influence for the first acid jazz groups. Even the Beastie Boys pay homage to Holmes on one of their albums. This is a popular setting Holmes used on his hit recording. The "Misty" setting added a few drawbars to Smith's configuration and employed the second percussion harmonic and the less-used C2 vibrato. On many of the examples you will notice we have the Leslie set to brake. This eliminates the slight chorus sound of the bass with the chorale setting. Some organists still prefer the slow spin; I almost always use the brake setting. I do like chorale for ballads or when I'm playing with a bassist.

The material for the right-hand lines comes mostly from major scales and arpeggios. In the last bar, we have a scalar passage that highlights the G and B of the D♭7♯11 chord. A note about bass lines: The material is the same as for the right-hand lines. The only difference is that the scales and chromatic notes are usually moving in quarter notes. This is why you will often see a bass note root on beat 1 and 3 and chromatic passing tones on beats 2 and 4. Again, we have two pedal walk-downs. Use the heel-to-toe like the previous examples.

 TIP 5

888640000   on/soft/fast/2nd   C2 Vib/Leslie brake

6 THE KEITH EMERSON SETTING

Keith Emerson is my biggest influence on organ. He is said to have become interested in the Hammond after hearing Jack McDuff's "Rock Candy." This is the classic Jimmy Smith setting with the percussion set to normal for more bite. Rather than a B3, Keith used a C3 and L100 with four Leslies driven by Custom Hiwatt 100 amplifiers to get some dirt in his sound. The bass line in our exercise is a prog rock drone in C minor. The pedals tap eighth notes. The right-hand improvisation comes from playing the notes of the C Dorian mode (C-D-Eb-F-G-A-Bb-C) in unusual intervals such as 2nds and 4ths. Notice how the lines quickly change direction and skip notes that were just played; this creates interesting intervalic shapes.

To really get this style of playing together, experiment with playing modes like Dorian and Mixolydian in 4ths as arpeggios and voicings. This will lead you to a whole new way of seeing the grid of a key. It's very important with this – as well as the other exercises – to figure out the pattern, then transpose the exercise to 12 keys. Freedom in improvisation comes from comfort with the entire system.

 TIP 6

888000000   on/norm/fast/3rd   C3 Vib/Leslie brake

THE STEVE WINWOOD SETTING

Steve Winwood was a seminal figure in the UK rock scene of the 1960s and '70s. He was a key member of several amazing bands, including the Spencer Davis Group, Traffic, and Blind Faith. As a session musician, his résumé includes some of the biggest names in music over the last 40 years. Winwood often used the interesting drawbar setting in this example. All the white bars are pulled out and the dark ones are set to 4. It's almost a classic tibia setting – we'll cover this in a few examples – with a little extra.

Steve was a powerful organist whose trademark was bluesy blasts with a swirling Leslie. Experiment with turning the Leslie from fast to slow or brake as you hold the chords. Our example shows diatonic chords and clusters from the E Mixolydian mode (E-F♯-G♯-A-B-C♯-D-E). It's common in this type of organ vamp to hold the top note with the pinky of the right hand while the other fingers outline chords underneath. Notice how you see a lot of A major triads. The IV-I harmonic motion is strong and can be used often within a riff. Try also combining other diatonic triads like E and F♯ minor for chordal and improvising ideas.

 TIP 7

848848448   perc off   C3 Vib/Leslie fast

THE ROD ARGENT SETTING

Here's another rock setting that uses the second percussion harmonic. The example below is highly influenced by Rod's blazing solo on "Time of the Season" by the Zombies. If you read between the lines, you'll start to see that the English rock organists internalized the American jazz style, distorted the sound, changed the groove, and arrived at their own ground-breaking Hammond techniques. In this example, the bass E is doubled in the pedals.

When you can play the exercise well, try comping on the lower manual with this setting: 00680000. This will shift the octave up just like the +1 octave key on more modern keyboards. With this registration, you can play chords underneath your right-hand lines in the style of a jazz pianist comping for his own solo. All the material for our solo comes from the E Dorian mode (E-F#-G-A-B-C#-D-E) and the E minor pentatonic scale (E-G-A-B-D-E). Only the first two drawbars are pulled out, with a strong second harmonic percussion. This gives our lines a clipped, muted feel. On your own, experiment with turning the Leslie from slow to fast and back.

 TIP 8

880000000   on/norm/fast/2nd   No Vib/Leslie brake

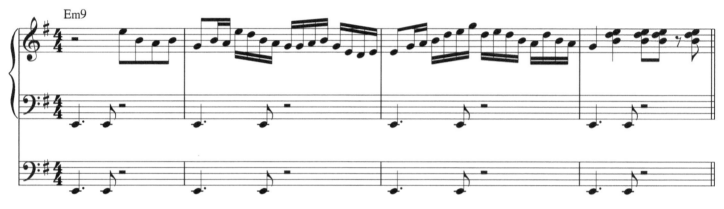

9 THE GOSPEL SETTING

This is a popular setting for a churchy, sanctified sound. The second, third, and fourth drawbars can be combined in many different ways, with the first and last drawbar all the way out to make slight variations of this sound. This setting works great when you need a singing solo line in an R&B or funk tune. The Leslie is switched from slow to fast according to taste. The notes in this exercise come from the G major pentatonic scale (G-A-B-D-E-G). Bars 3 and 4 have alternating G major and A minor triads in different inversions, harmonizing a pentatonic riff. You often see this technique of mixing the triads of the first two diatonic chords in a key in gospel organ playing.

The bass line is a doo-wop ostinato with the pedals pumping. Use the volume pedal to create gentle volume swells so the line sings like a voice. Switch the Leslie fast/slow to taste. I take the brake off for this one, too. The slow spin of the chorale is really nice on this setting. Also of note is how much mileage we get from simple pentatonic scales. They are easy to remember, and often work over a whole progression of chords. When you get this example under your fingers, experiment switching to the G minor pentatonic scale (G-B♭-C-D-F-G), this time alternating G minor and A minor triads.

TIP 9

888000008   perc off   C3 Vib/Leslie fast

This is a nice color to use once in a while – on a ballad or after a very big shout section. This setting has all the drawbars pushed in and uses just the sound of the second percussion harmonic. The volume of the percussion is set to normal for maximum click. If you need more volume, try pulling out the fourth drawbar just a bit to bolster the sound. Our riff is a simple F blues lick (F-Ab-Bb-B-C-Eb-F) that repeats. The plinky sound of the percussion makes cutesy little riffs like this sound great.

The bass line again uses notes from the F and Bb Mixolydian scales with a few chromatic embellishments. The pedals pump with an occasional heel-to-toe walk-up, like the end of bar 1. Usually, when playing the percussion-only setting, the second harmonic is used because the third harmonic creates a pitch a 5th above the note that will make you sound like you are in a different key. Hey wait… that sounds cool, actually.

 TIP 10

000000000   on/norm/fast/2nd   C3 Vib/Leslie brake

11 THE JON LORD SETTING

Jon Lord, another giant of English rock organ, played his Hammond with a straight and heavily distorted sound. This was achieved by taking an output directly from the organ and putting it through a powerful guitar amp like a Marshall. To emulate this sound, the vibrato should be off and the Leslie on brake. If you have a B3 clone keyboard, there is usually a distortion knob you can use to get the sound. Most of these keyboards even come with Jon Lord patches.

The bass line is a quarter-note stomp with the pedals pumping. Try toe-to-heel this time on the B to C walk-up. You will see in the music example that we mix some major 3rds with our C minor pentatonic riff. The distortion and straight sound make the subtle harmonic change and the blue notes voiced in 4ths a prog rock star's dream come true. Turn the distortion almost all the way up on your clone and select a Marshall or comparable British amp setting.

 TIP 11

888800000   perc off   No Vib/Leslie brake   effect: overdrive

12 THE PROCUL HAREM SETTING

The Summer of Love had a great anthem in 1967 with Procul Harem's debut single, "A Whiter Shade of Pale." Organist Matt Fisher originally played a Hammond M102, but we can easily get our B3 to emulate the sound. Pull the first, fourth, and sixth drawbars all the way out, with no vibrato or percussion. Even though the lads used bass in '67, we will supply our own just to practice our pedals on the simple descending line.

The harmonic motion of this example is a Bach-inspired major scale with harmonized triads in inversions played by the left hand on the lower manual. Again, our two lowest drawbars in the bottom manual are pushed in with only the third one out to 7. This puts the range of the keyboard up an octave and makes it so our chords can fit snugly beneath the right-hand melody on top. Right before the downbeat of bar 2, switch the Leslie to fast then go right back to comping chords. The notes of the right-hand melody all come from the C major scale.

 TIP 12

Upper Manual: 800808000   perc off   No Vib/Leslie fast/slow
Lower Manual: 007000000

13 THE SOULFUL SETTING

This is another setting popularized by Groove Holmes. The upper drawbars give this registration a nice sparkle. Use the Leslie liberally with this sound, too. In this example, I've supplied a funky left-hand bass line in the style of Bootsy Collins. Notice how the bass pedals still just pump on the downbeat. You can mix other accents in the pedals if you like. Experiment to come up with your own style. (Chester Thompson of Tower of Power would go toe/heel on the same pedal to get repetitive 16th-note bass lines.)

It takes a bit of practice to get your right-hand lines to sound relaxed against the syncopated bass line. Just practice slowly and with a metronome. Our solo material is from the D blues (D-F-G-A-C-D) and D Mixolydian (D-E-F♯-G-A-B-C-D) scales. Notice that in bar 3 we mix notes from D major and C major triads. On a dominant 7th chord, practice arpeggiating the tonic and ♭7 major triads on top of each other. This is called the hexatonic approach; we will speak more about it later.

 TIP 13

Upper Manual: 888804664   perc off   No Vib/Leslie fast/slow

14 THE NEW JAZZ SETTING

This registration is a variation on the original Jimmy Smith setting. It has a little more sparkle and whistle with the addition of the fourth and eighth drawbar. Joey D often uses this setting, as do many other modern organists. I've selected the slow percussion decay for this sound, to create a slightly more legato effect. It works great with fast bebop.

The lines come from a combination of arpeggios and scales. Notice how the notes in our improvisations outline the chord alterations and important notes like 3rds and roots. In beats 3 and 4 of bar 1, for instance, a descending G+ arpeggio creates a great line with unusual intervals. Bar 2 also starts with an arpeggio, an E♭maj7 chord over the C bass note. When we put a B minor triad on top of the F bass note on beat 3 of bar 2, we get interesting alterations of ♯11 and ♭9.

Super Tip: Always be on the lookout for an advanced application of a simple thing. You know what to do now: 12 keys. Play a minor triad a tritone above the root for a cool F7♯11(♭9) sound – then up a 5th (or 4th) again and again until you are back where you started.

 TIP 14

Upper Manual: 888400050   on/soft/slow/3rd   C3 Vib/Leslie brake

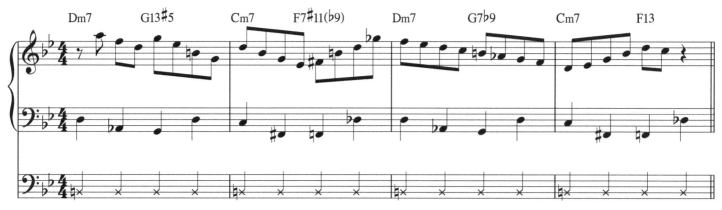

THE ETHEL SMITH SETTING

The original Latin from Manhattan, Ethel Smith represented the Hammond Organ Company in the early days. After impressing a dealer with her playing, she convinced him to let her use the then-new instrument on a Florida Trio gig. Smith often toured Central and Latin America, where she developed a great fondness for Latin music. At the height of the 1940s Latin music craze, Smith scored a huge hit with "Tico Tico" and even had a cameo appearance in the 1944 film *Bathing Beauty*.

In this example, over the simple Latin root-5th bass motion and pumping pedal, the right hand arpeggiates chords for soloing. Over the E7♭9 chord, diminished 7th voicings move in minor 3rds to provide some cool symmetrical runs. Notice the trick: Over a 7♭9 chord you can play a diminished 7th chord a half step above the bass note. In other words, over E7♭9 play Fdim7 for solo ideas and for a great voicing. This drawbar registration is referred to as the tibia setting. It's a popular church setting with a rather consonant sound. The F♯ in the last arpeggio adds a nice minor 13th color. Leslie on fast and mambo, baby!

 TIP 15

Upper Manual: 808808008   perc off   C3 Vib/Leslie fast

 THE CLARINET SETTING

This is another Ethel Smith setting from "Tico Tico." It's a reedy sound because of the use of the darker drawbars. It's also an octave higher because the sub drawbars are both pushed in. We'll turn the Leslie to slow so we get a little gentle chorusing to add movement. Again, our solo material is made up of triads with a few colorful notes like the Cmaj7 on beat 1 of bar 3 and the F6 in the last bar.

When you are on a real B3, it's fun to set up one of the top manuals like this and have a more generic drawbar setting on the other manual. You switch between the two using the B and B♭ keys in the group of preset keys with reverse colors to the left of the two manuals. Think ahead while you are on a gig to plan for sounds that you could switch to later in a song. With a little planning, you can use the unlimited sonic potential of the B3 to create interesting arcs in a piece of music.

 TIP 16

Upper Manual: 007373430   perc off   C3 Vib/Leslie chorale

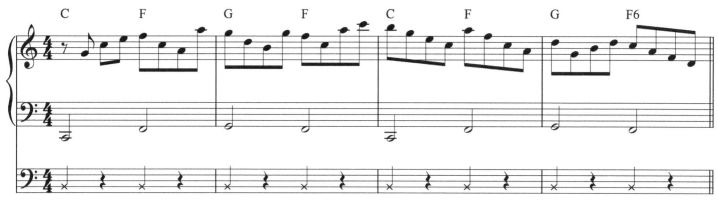

17 THE LARRY GOLDINGS SETTING #1

A few years ago, organist Larry Goldings was featured in a popular music magazine article. In it, he spoke about some unusual drawbar settings he liked.

Two of them really caught my attention. The first one has the second, fourth, and sixth drawbars pulled all the way out. This setting creates a lot of unusual overtones because of the intervals created by the dissonant bars.

Play your voicings rather low on the top manual, and with small chords so that the strange intervals have a chance to peak out. In our example, we comp simple two-note chords that sound like they have more mysterious notes because of our unusual setting. The simple bass line chugs along with pumping bass pedals as usual. Try to walk a few more real lines with the pedals as your confidence starts to grow. Try this kind of vamp at the end of a bluesy shuffle as the saxophonist walks the bar.

 TIP 17

Upper Manual: 080808000   perc off   No Vib/Leslie brake

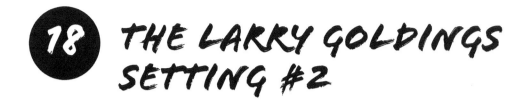

THE LARRY GOLDINGS SETTING #2

This registration is called the "triad setting." Like the last example, it's meant to be played in a lower octave on the top manual. This time, the second, seventh, and eighth bars are pulled all the way out, making slightly different overtones than the previous example. I like to switch between these two settings to add a little slow development to a riff. Again, arpeggios save the day in the right hand. The dissonant intervals of the dark bars give our simple lines an other-worldly feel. Go toe-to-heel in the walk-down at the end of bar 2. Notice the triplet in bar 3. Bebop players often toss a triplet figure into the middle of a scalar passage for a little rhythmic interest.

 TIP 18

Upper Manual: 080000880   perc off   No Vib/Leslie brake

19 THE COUNTRY SETTING

This registration will come in handy on a Nashville recording session. It has the first two and last three bars pulled out in a half moon shape. The example below has the setting 850000357, but you can make small adjustments to get the flavor you like. The beauty of this registration is that it provides color in the low and high frequencies and leaves the middle open for the guitars and vocals to do their thing.

This is another instance where we will play bass entirely with our feet. The left-hand comps on the lower manual with a setting that has the first two bars pushed all the way in – such as 005730000. Country music has lots of grace notes, especially from the 2nd to 3rd scale degree. Our first riff has one. The sound mimics the pedal steel and gives a nod to a great country music pianist, Floyd Cramer. The solo lines are all major scales derived from the root of each chord. For that authentic country waltz sound, add a little lilt to the rhythmic feel.

 TIP 19

Upper Manual: 850000357   perc off   C3 Vib/Leslie fast

20 THE SILK SETTING

Here's another effective setting for country music. Pull out the first, third, and last drawbar and use liberal Leslie. A nice variation of this sound is to push in the third bar, which makes an even more hollow sound. Also experiment with different bars like the fourth and sixth for more settings and variation. This registration sounds great on all Leslie speeds, and I often switch between brake, chorale, and fast – frequently. We keep the same country-inspired chords and bass from the last example. Our right hand has the "Silk Setting" and a few more rhythmic tricks. Everything else is still just major scales with an occasional grace note.

 TIP 20

Upper Manual: 808000008   perc off   C3 Vib/Leslie fast

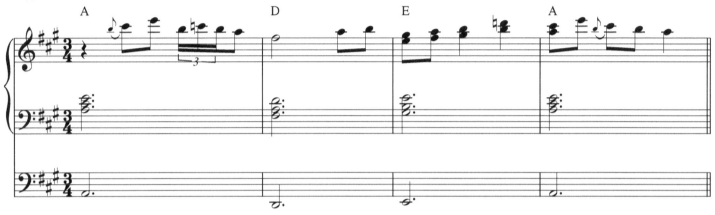

21 THE LARRY YOUNG SETTING

Larry Young is probably the most important post-Jimmy Smith jazz organist. He has developed a whole new language for improvising. Taking a cue from mid-1960s jazz pianists like McCoy Tyner and Chick Corea, Young started to use mostly 4ths for his solos and chords. In our example, all the notes in the treble clef are from the F Mixolydian scale (F-G-A-B♭-C-D-E♭-F); they are just played in 4th shapes. This can be clearly seen in bar 3. Bar 1 shows a common Young device: arpeggiating a tonic (F) and ♭VII (E♭) triad to get a great, open F7 sound. Notice also that Young preferred the unusual C1 vibrato setting.

 TIP 21

Upper Manual: 888000000   perc on/soft/fast/3rd   C1 Vib/Leslie brake

22 THE JESSE CRAWFORD SETTING

Jesse Crawford was a theatre organist who became famous for playing during the silent movies of the 1920s. Jesse used many different settings, but the one we've chosen sounds great with chords and is one that many attribute to him. In this example, we play a simple chordal solo over a I-VI-II-V progression. Please pardon the F♭s and A♯s; there's no easy way to write these passing chords, which in most cases are diminished 7th shapes that alternate with inside tonal shapes. Take a look at beat 1 in bar 2: What we could call a C♯dim 7 chord (even though it's spelled a little differently) leads effectively to the Dm7 voicing in the next beat. For practice, try voicing your own melodies with simple chords. Use those diminished shapes on notes that aren't chord tones. Notice at the end of bar 3 how the melody is harmonized with diminished chords, again resolving to Dm7 (bar 4, beat 1).

TIP 22

Upper Manual: 800800000   perc off   C3 Vib/Leslie fast

23 THE BRIAN AUGER SETTING

British rock/jazz organist Brian Auger has played with lots of great artists, including Hendrix and Zeppelin. He also formed his own groundbreaking band, Brian Auger's Oblivion Express, in 1970. The example below uses the second harmonic and a normal percussion level – for a little more snap and click on 16th-note Em pentatonic scale (E-G-A-B-D-E) riffs. The bass line comes from the same scale. It's a little tricky to play a syncopated bass line like this while playing the solo. Practice really slowly; eventually, you will begin to feel it in your body. Try to get your pedals to follow the rhythm of the bass line. It's okay to fudge a little. Don't hesitate to tap only downbeats if you get off. Just stay relaxed.

 TIP 23

Upper Manual: 888110000   perc on/norm/fast/2nd   C3 Vib/Leslie chorale

THE CHARLES EARLAND SETTING

Also known as The Mighty Burner, Philly native Charles Earland was a tenor saxophonist with Jimmy McGriff before switching to organ to jam with Pat Martino and Lou Donaldson. Charles liked to use four drawbars out with the third percussion harmonic. The second bar can also be pulled out to 8, but here we keep it at 4. The shuffle bass line plugs along as the right hand plays spiffy riffs from the D blues scale (D-F-G-Ab-A-C-D). In the pedals, go toe-to-heel on the walk-downs. Notice how we use minor 2nd intervals and grace notes around the blue note (Ab) to get the funk.

TIP 24

Upper Manual: 848800000   perc on/soft/fast/3rd   C3 Vib/Leslie brake

THE OBOE SETTING

This is one of the settings from the original Hammond owner's manual. The two bass drawbars on the top manual are pushed in so the line will sound like it's played in a higher register. We also use a snaky V3 vibrato. V3 puts a great vibe on a melismatic line à la Korla Pandit. The right-hand lines are comprised mostly of arpeggios with a few scale tones – in bar 1 from C Dorian mode and in bar 2 from the E♭ major scale. The left hand and pedals play a simple bass line with the pedal sounding on the downbeat of each bar, then just taps.

TIP 25

Upper Manual: 004632100   perc off   V3 Vib/Leslie brake

THE "AMAZING GRACE" SETTING

This drawbar registration sounds great in gospel music. In this example, we will have the pedals mirror the left hand. Take your left hand off the bottom manual to switch the Leslie to fast in the second bar. The right-hand chords are simple triads for churchy sounds. Notice the doubled 3rds in bar 2; this stacking sounds good with these shapes. The top and bottom voices move in contrary motion.

 TIP 26

Upper Manual: 468642468   perc off   C3 Vib/Leslie slow/fast

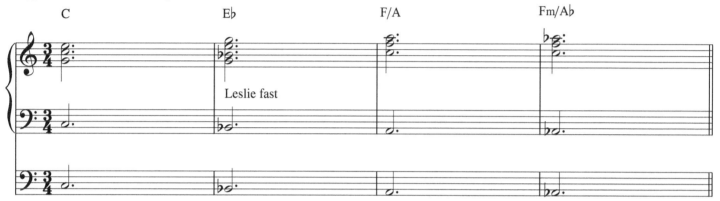

THE "BORN TO BE WILD" SETTING

This comes from the epic Steppenwolf song and is a terrific setting for rock tunes. In our example below, we rock out on the pedals and left hand with a I-IV progression while the right hand plays classic rock chords. You'll want to practice this lick in all keys, for sure. You can also try switching the Leslie to different speeds for slight variance.

TIP 27

Upper Manual: 888643200   perc off   C3 Vib/Leslie fast

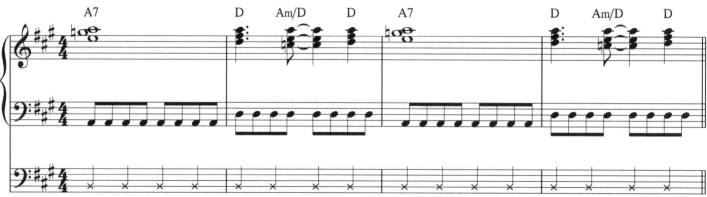

28 THE XYLOPHONE SETTING

Here's another classic from the original Hammond manual. Try sneaking this one in once a night when you want to shock the audience. With the pedals tapping, the harmony moves in a iii-vi-ii-V turnaround while the right hand highlights the 7ths moving to the 3rds. Because the sub drawbars are pushed in, this will sound in a register higher than it's played. For another color, try switching the vibrato to a V3 setting.

 TIP 28

Upper Manual: 000800080   perc on/norm/slow/2nd   C3 Vib/Leslie break

29 THE BALLAD SETTING

This is a great registration for playing ballads. To add a level of difficulty, we've moved the exercise to the challenging key of B major. The pedals hit the first note of the bar and tap for the other notes. The right hand spins a groovy line with fast Leslie. The notes in our improvisation come mostly from arpeggios, with a few connecting notes. Notice how the E at the end of bar 1 resolves to the F♯ of bar 2. In your improvisations, look for simple ways to connect chord tones in a progression you are trying to play over.

 TIP 29

Upper Manual: 800000008   perc off   C3 Vib/Leslie fast

30  THE DIAPASON SETTING

Here's another from the original Hammond manual. This setting has a hollow higher sound because the first bars are pushed in and the middle bars gently slope. We have a triplety blues solo that hovers around a C major pentatonic scale (C-D-E-G-A-C). This scale works great over the whole blues. Combine it with the C minor blues scale (C-E♭-F-F♯-G-B♭-C) for a great one-two punch on every blues tune.

 TIP 30

Upper Manual: 005521000 perc off C3 Vib/Leslie chorale

31 BLACK PRESET KEY WAH-WAH

Here's a useful trick for a Reggae tune. As you are playing a solo on the upper manual with your right hand, start switching between the preset keys to the left of the manual while holding down the lowest cancel key. The presets were some original Hammond settings that could be "programmed" with lots of solder. For this trick, randomly switch between the preset keys with the fingers of your left hand while continuing to play your solo line for a wah-wah type effect.

32 THE REGGAE BUBBLE

This is the classic organ comping part when you want to "rasta reggae down, mon." The drawbar settings are hollow sounding with a chorale speed on the Leslie. Stay loose to hit all these offbeats. For effect, add some windmill chops. (See Tip 33.) The interlocking parts provide an undulating feel for the drop-one beat in the drums. The lower manual has the sub bars pushed in to raise the range and give the illusion of overlapping hands

 TIP 32

Upper Manual: 800000008   perc off   C3 Vib/Leslie chorale
Lower Manual: 008400004

manuals only

33 WINDMILL CHOPS

On the bottom manual, pull out the third drawbar (00800000) and gliss both hands over each other, smashing in all the keys up and down the keyboard. This is a Keith Emerson fav; with some reverb and distortion it sounds sloppy and killer. The beauty of the Hammond waterfall keys is you can smash and smear till you plotz.

34 UNPLUG THE WHITE CORDS

If your Leslie switch doesn't have a brake setting, you can unplug the white cables from the amp on the Leslie to stop the slow motors. In the front of the amp, on the bottom of your Leslie speaker, there are two brown and two white electrical cords. These are the fast and slow motor controls. Pull the white ones out of the sockets, and the Leslie will brake. Because it's a more direct sound, jazz players often prefer the brake setting when they have to walk bass lines.

35 THE SYMMETRY OF THE DIMINISHED SCALE

The beauty of the diminished scale is that you can play the same material in minor 3rds for great soloing ideas. Let's look at soloing over C7♯9. We will use the half-step/whole-step diminished scale (C-D♭-E♭-E-F♯-G-A-B♭). If we play major and minor triads moving in minor 3rds, we get the same notes as are in the diminished scale. The left-hand chords are also ♯9 voicings moving in minor 3rds. Play these as arpeggios in your right hand for more solo ideas. In the last two bars, I've given you a few soloing ideas by combining the triads.

 TIP 35

Upper Manual: 888800000   Lower Manual: 008400008   other settings as you like

34

36 THE BEBOP SCALES

These scales were made famous by Charlie Parker. (As a side note, I highly recommend picking up a copy of the *Omnibook*, which has Bird's solos transcribed. It was my Bible when I was a kid.) The bebop scales are basically major and minor scales with a few chromatic notes. They are usually played in a descending direction and often approached by quickly ascending arpeggios. Notice that the major and minor bebop scales have only one different note: the 3rd.

 TIP 36

Upper Manual: 888800000   Lower Manual: 008400008   other settings as you like

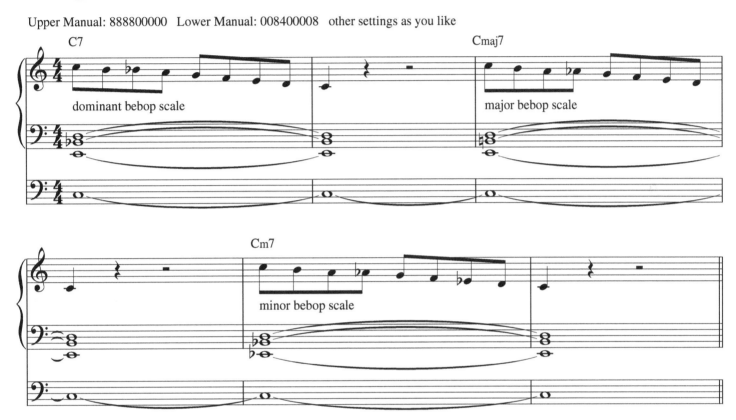

37 TURNING THE THING ON

Here's the proper procedure for starting a Hammond organ: Hold the start switch for eight seconds; you will hear the tone generator begin to turn. After eight seconds, continue holding the start switch and turn on the "run" switch. Continue to hold both switches on for another four seconds.

38 PITCH BEND

If you are rocking out and need that little extra to put you over the edge, try this: With the organ already running, press the "start" switch. This makes the generator speed up, which causes the pitch to go up. Conversely, switching the "run" switch off and on quickly gives a downward pitch bend. These are neat tricks for a little prog rock madness, but I'm sure it's not great for the organ.

39 THE HARLEM DOWN-AND-DIRTY PEDALS 101 COURSE

People often make a lot bigger deal about pedals than they need to. The simplest way to start playing pedals is to pull the first pedal drawbar out to 7 and start "tapping" the B in the middle of the pedal staff with a flat foot in the rhythm of the left-hand bass line. Try to hit the pedal very lightly so that the note does not fully sound. We're looking for the attack at the beginning of the sound, before the note develops. When you start playing pedals, you will probably get tired easily. Just take breaks when you run out of gas and walk with your left hand alone. Eventually, you will be able to do it all night. As you get more comfortable, start taking chances: pedal a note here and there, play pedals on ballads, comp on the lower manual as you play all bass on the pedals during a bridge. Try to play short lines and turnarounds with your feet by switching from heel to toe.

40 THE HARLEM FIRST-SET HEEL THUMP

Thumping pedals at a really fast tempo can be exhausting. Sometimes if the tempo is too fast, I will rest my toe on the wood in front of the pedals and thump the B♭ with my heel. It's pretty easy to get a relaxed sound this way. Remember to keep your body loose; don't muscle it.

41 THE HARLEM LAST-SET TOE TAP

Organist Adam Scone told me about this when I was playing long sessions at a great spot in Harlem called Showmans Jazz Club. When your tapping leg is exhausted after a long night, rest your left thigh on the corner of the bench and tap the low C with your toe. The idea is to hang your leg freely like you're a kid on a swing. This lets the upper part of your leg rest.

42 MINOR PENTATONIC FOR MINOR 7TH CHORDS

For Tips 42–44, we will be talking about using overlapping minor pentatonic scales to create interesting lines in improvisations. Here we will combine three scales: C minor pentatonic, D minor pentatonic, and G minor pentatonic for use over Cmin7. By mixing notes from these three scales, we get interesting lines automatically. The only thing going on is our head should be: "Over minor 7th chords, play the minor pentatonic of the I, II, and V." Think only of the roots of the scales, but switch from one to the other and back quickly and see and feel the shapes that leap out. Play this one in 12 keys, for sure.

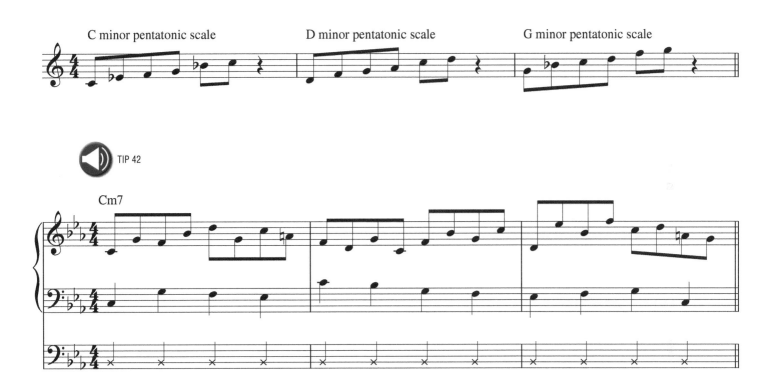

43 MINOR PENTATONIC FOR MAJOR 7TH CHORDS

In this example we will combine E minor pentatonic, A minor pentatonic, and B minor pentatonic for use over Cmaj7. The only thing going on is our head should be: "Over major 7th chords, play the minor pentatonic of the III, VI, and VII." Notice the cool ♯11 sound in the B minor pentatonic.

 TIP 43

44 MINOR PENTATONIC FOR DOMINANT 7TH CHORDS

The example below combines D minor pentatonic, G minor pentatonic, and A minor pentatonic for use over C7. The only thing going on is our head should be, "Over dominant 7th chords, play the minor pentatonic of the II, V, VI." In Tips 42–44, the pedals tap and the bass line follows the scale of each chord.

45 THE INSEN SCALE

The Insen scale is a Japanese scale popularized by McCoy Tyner; he especially liked to use it over m7♭5 chords. If you play the D Insen scale a 4th above the root chord of Am7♭5, you get a great-sounding exotic pentatonic. I've given you a few more applications in the remainder of the exercise. The left-hand chords are played low on the bottom manual and are transposed up two octaves because the first three drawbars are pushed in.

 TIP 45

Lower Manual: 000806008

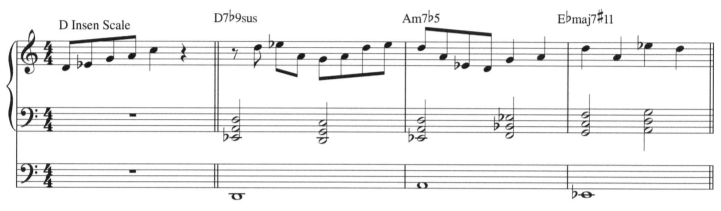

46 THE HIRAJOSHI SCALE

I'm always on the hunt for strange scales from around the world. I try to notice the shapes and then apply them to jazz chords, so while we're at it, here are a few more Japanese scales. I've given you a few examples. Try to find your own applications.

47 HUNGARIAN MAJOR AND MINOR SCALES

I spend a lot of time in Eastern Europe and have developed a fondness for these two scales. When I want to step out of the box in the middle of a solo, I start playing them, using the minor one for minor chords and the major one for dominant chords. Try using V3 vibrato, too. It will give these scales an exotic, ethnic flavor.

C Hungarian minor scale   C Hungarian major scale

48 VOICE CHORDS IN 4THS

Harmonize modes in 4ths to get a Larry Young sound in your chord voicings. Instead of playing one note at a time, stack two other 4th intervals (or aug4th, depending on the mode) on top of the original scale. All the resulting voicings can be used for comping or when broken into arpeggios, soloing on the corresponding chord. In bar 1, our harmonized 4th shapes work great for comping over Cm7. In the next two bars, Mixolydian and Ionian modes are covered. Also experiment slipping up and down a half step to give a little chromaticism to your comping. In the last bar, I've given some 4th shapes à la Larry Young. These work great for Cm7 and for B7#9 as well.

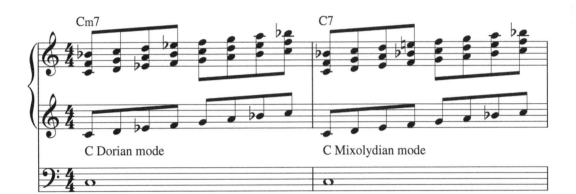

C Dorian mode   C Mixolydian mode

C Ionian mode   McCoy voicings

I was lucky enough to study with Charlie Banacos, a great piano teacher in Boston. Charlie loved to take triads from scales and combine them as overlapping arpeggios for soloing ideas. This technique is sometimes referred to as the "hexatonic" approach. In the example below I've listed four scales and have taken some triads from scales. Look for your own or combine three for soloing ideas. The cool thing about this style is that you are thinking of simple triads that automatically make cool lines with interesting intervals.

Triads F + E♭ or
Gm + Adim
=F7

Triads Gm + A♭ or
Cm + Fm
=Fm7

Triads G + Am or
G + C
=Fmaj7#11

Triads F + A♭ or
Bm + Dm
=F7alt

50 ANOTHER GURU

Kenny Werner was my other big Guru, even though I studied with him only for a short time. Maybe you've heard of his popular book *Effortless Mastery.* Back when I studied with Kenny, we practiced a thing called The Five-Finger Exercise, which consisted of effortlessly dropping your fingers one at a time on the keyboard with no judgment or care of what it sounds like or even if a key goes down. The exercise reprograms how you feel about the instrument, how it feels, and how the baggage you bring from your life doesn't matter. Check out Kenny Werner!

51 COMPING

This continues our discussion in Tip 48. The 4th voicings from bars 1–3 are all notes from the B♭ major scale. If we harmonize the scale in 4ths, we have many possibilities for interesting voicings to play. Try to make small melodies with the top note of your voicing and look for shapes that work well over each chord. The last bar harmonizes the G altered scale (G-A♭-B♭-C♭-D♭-E♭-F-G). You can also think of this as an A♭ melodic minor over a G bass note. On your own, try playing all your fancy scales in 4ths for lots of chords.

 TIP 51

Lower Manual: 838000000   no perc/C3 Vibrato

PEDALS ON BALLADS

When you start to feel comfortable with the pedals, start playing bass notes on some ballads. The lower manual is set to comp in a great range with the setting 000805000. The pedals sound on beats 1 and 3. You can basically use your toe or heel or a combination of the two to get around on the pedals. Sit up straight and discover what "fingerings" work best on the feet. The right-hand lines are mostly broken-chord voicings. Notice how the D minor triplet line works well as it resolves sensibly to D♭maj7. Try this exercise with other ballads you like to play.

 TIP 52

Upper Manual: 8080000008   Lower Manual: 000805000   Vibrato and Leslie to taste

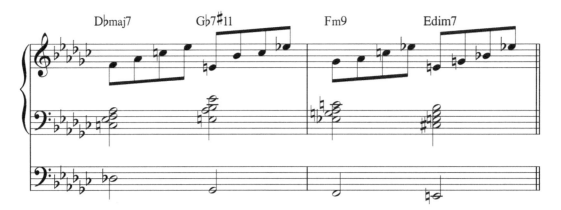

53 JON LORD 4TH ENDING

This is a fun one at the end of a rock tune, courtesy of Jon Lord. (See Tip 11.) Take the major tonic (I) chord and move the major 3rd up a half step for this crunchy stab. Turn the distortion up, Leslie brake, no vibrato, percussion if you like, first four drawbars out.

 TIP 53

88880000   No Vibrato/No Leslie   lots of distortion

54 JON LORD HARMONIC MINOR

While we're speaking about Jon, let's look at how he liked to play a descending harmonic minor riff. The scale has a ♭6 and a ♮7, which provide its distinctive sound (E-F#-G-A-B-C-D#-E). The riff starts on tonic and plays a sequence of four notes that goes down each note of the scale. Keep the distortion turned up and use the same setting as the last example.

 TIP 54

Upper Manual: 88880000   No Vibrato/No Leslie   lots of distortion

55 TWO MANUAL LINES

This is a good trick to get rapid-fire lines. We set the lower manual an octave up so the hands sound like they are on top of each other. Here we chose a similar consonant drawbar sound for both manuals, but we don't have to. In the example, the right hand follows the left by an eighth note. This gives the illusion that we are striking the same key twice. Experiment on your own playing two manual lines with all black keys on the bottom and all white keys on top (or vice versa) to create super overlapping lines.

 TIP 55

Upper Manual: 008088000   Lower Manual: 000808000   all other settings to taste

56 THE SQUABBLE BLACK-KEY SLAP

While you are squabbling, no matter what key you are in, slap the black keys in a descending smear in the middle of your solo.

57 DON'T VIBE ME

The vibrato/chorus scanner can be used to get a huge variety of organ sounds: C1 – Larry Young; C3 – Jimmy Smith; C2 – Groove Holmes; no vibrato – Mel Rhyne; V3 – Lonnie Smith for snaky sounds. Switch up your vibratos for different colors. Some players always use vibrato on the lower manual to beef up the bass.

58 LOWER-MANUAL GOSPEL

If you go to a Baptist church, you may be lucky enough to hear a great gospel organist. When the preacher is speaking, the organist accompanies him by playing big two-handed chords on the lower manual, with bass pedals. The top manual is used for accents and big shouts when needed. Notice the use of 9ths and 11ths in the chords below. Because the bass line is covered in the feet, church organists can play lush, smeary chords. Use a slow Leslie speed for poignant testifying.

 TIP 58

Lower Manual: 0088880000   C3 Vib/Leslie Slow

59 THE MATCH BOOK TRICK

When I was first starting to play organ, I remember hearing stories about organists of old who would wedge a matchbook between the keys to keep a note depressed while they worked out some licks below. I have to admit, I've never tried it, but on occasion I will hold a key with the top or bottom finger while I play above or below the held note. In the first two bars below, the pinky holds the C while the other fingers play a riff in the style of Jimmy Smith underneath. The last two bars flip the script; the thumb holds middle C while the top fingers play the blues.

 TIP 59

Upper Manual: 808808008   C3 Vib/Leslie slow/fast

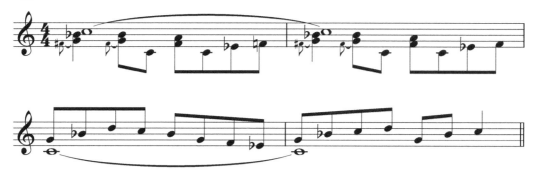

60 THUMB SLIDE IN LINE

This one is hard to notate, so check out some older online vids of Jimmy Smith. You will notice that sometimes, in the middle of a fast line, he will do a short upward glissando with his thumb over the white keys and then go right back to playing his line. The organ sounds so great when you are a little sloppy.

61 PUSH IN LOW BARS WHILE PLAYING

Try to do this at the same time as you are doing the thumb slide from Tip 60: While playing a right-hand solo with a little thumb glissando, use your left hand to push in all the low bars quickly – to get the glassy partials to sound – then pull them right back out.

FOUR FAMILY SHAPES

When selecting a drawbar tone, it's sometimes helpful to have one of the following patterns in mind as a starting point for tone selection:

008500000   Flute Family

008776543   Diapason Family

004676543   Reed Family (triangle pattern)

004555543   String Family (bow pattern)

Notice the shape of the drawbars. When playing with your own group, try to dial up some of these original Hammond Owner's Manual shapes. They offer interesting alternatives to the stock modern settings.

63 C.T. BASS PUMP

The first time I really understood the power of the B3 was when I heard Chester Thompson play with Tower of Power. This example focuses on an interesting bass technique Chester made famous on the TOP tune "Squibb Cakes." The left foot bounces between heel and toe on the same pedal while the thumb and third finger mimic the line in the left hand. This is pretty difficult to get at first. Make sure you stay relaxed. To start, you can play only quarter notes in the pedals. On top, we have a Chesteresque riff from the C blues scale that repeats every six 16th notes, creating an interesting hemiola as the bass chugs along.

 TIP 63

Upper Manual: 888800008   C3 Vib/Leslie slow/fast
Lower Manual: 838000000   Pedals: 70

64 LOWER MANUAL BLUES

On a medium blues tune, sometimes it's nice to play your solo on the lower manual so that the bass line and solo line have the same setting. Jimmy Smith did this every once-in-a-while as a chill alternative to his normal percussive settings.

SLOW DECAY

The most classic use of percussion is to have all the tabs up, which includes a fast percussion decay. For a slightly different sound, try switching the decay to slow. You will get a more legato sound. Slow decay also works very well with the second percussion harmonic. Here's one of my favorite settings: 888800000 no vibrato, Leslie brake on/norm/slow/second.

TWO-HANDED FUNK

When comping in a funk style, I like to come up with 16th-note interlocking parts to accentuate different portions of the beat. Here's a funk vamp in C minor with the pedals and left hand playing every 16th note that the right-hand comp is not playing. This creates an undulating feeling that works great against a straight-up funk beat in the drums. If you have a bass player in your band, you can substitute chords in the left hand for the bass notes, with the lower two drawbars pushed in.

 TIP 66

Upper Manual: 808000008   C3 Vib/Leslie brake/perc off
Lower Manual: 808000000   Pedals: 70

 **67** *TRIPLET SLAP*

Here's another funk tip. Try to play slapping accents with your left hand in the middle beats of your comping. This sounds great with the Leslie set to fast. In the bar below, we have basic descending diatonic chords in the F Dorian mode (F-G- A♭-B♭-C-D-E♭-F) with a few slapping accents played with the left hand.

 TIP 67

Upper Manual: 808000008   C3 Vib/Leslie fast/perc off

 68 *WHERE TO OIL*

When oiling your B3, the most important thing to remember: Use only Hammond oil. Look at the enclosed picture of the chassis. To the left you will see the motor/scanner assembly. The felt inside this "tub" should be damp with oil. Don't fill this one up, though, because it could cause glitches with the vibrato scanner. On the tone generator there are two more funnels that should be filled twice each. You should oil the organ periodically, but be careful not to do it too much. Some models have the oil cups in a different place, and some even have additional cups, so make sure you read up on your model to see about its specific oiling needs.

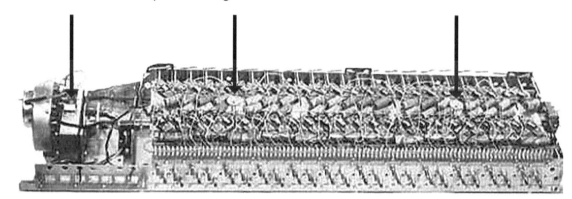

69 *USE A DOLLY*

If you are going to be moving your B3 around, you will benefit greatly from the use of dollies. Place one truck at each end of the B3, fasten the straps, and step on the foot levers on each side to raise the organ. You will find that your Hammond rolls around pretty easily. These are a must-have for moving an organ. With the help of a friend, I once pushed a B3 on dollies down Frenchman Street in New Orleans, so these things work well. Some guys can even do the moving from a van to a club by themselves.

 PENT SKIP NOTE

This is a technique often used by Boston jazz saxophonists. When playing a descending pentatonic lick, skip the second note. This skipped note becomes the first note in the new pattern. You can also make two skips.

 DRAWBAR DIFFERENCES

White: The fundamental tone. Pulling out subsequent white bars adds the tone up an octave: 008808008.

Black: These pitches are 3rds and 5ths to the fundamental. They are more nasal and dissonant: 000080880.

Brown: These are the left two bars in the manual and have the lowest sounds. The first drawbar is the fundamental tone down an octave, the 5 1/3 bar is the third harmonic of the first drawbar: 880000000.

 TRICK WITH LAST BAR AND PERCUSSION

On the percussion manual, some players pull out the last drawbar because it's inactivated when the percussion switch is on. By turning off the percussion switch, you instantly have a great funk setting without moving any drawbars.

 I GOT THE SHAKES

Whether playing two notes or four, you can shake your right-hand chords with fast Leslie for great smeary, sloppy deliciousness. The next time you hit a stab, stay in there and shake it all about. You do the hokey pokey and you…

74 DIMINISHED MAJOR 9TH CHORD

In a ballad, it's nice sometimes to sneak in a diminished major 9th chord. It works great at the top of a form as the last chord of a tune. For example, over a C bass note, play this voicing: Cdim(maj9). In the first half note, we show the voicing; its resolution (if you like) is given on the second chord.

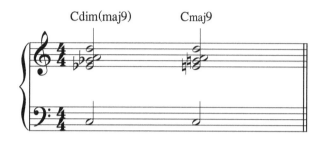

75 JAZZ LAYOUT

This is a great starting place for a B3 gig. You'll be set up to do just about anything from this template.

- Left-most manual: 808000006 for glassy comping on the top manual.

- Percussion manual: 888000000; all percussion tabs up.

- Bass Pedals: 70.

- 1st lower manual setting: 838000000 for bass lines.

- Last manual to the right: 008050000 for transposed chords if you have a bassist.

- Put your Leslie to brake.

- Vibrato on both manuals set to C3.

76 MY DIMINISHED SCALE

I say mine, but I'm not really sure. At some point in my musical travels, I noticed that if I combined the first three notes of a minor pentatonic scale with another that started on the note a tritone above the first note, I had a scale that I could use to improvise over diminished chords. This is a symmetrical scale, so you can repeat it at minor 3rd intervals. Look at the musical example and you can see it in action. If you move the root down a half step, this is also a great device that works over altered 7th chords Think: "Over B7alt play Brian's diminished trick starting on C."

 TIP 76

Upper Manual: 888800008   Lower Manual: 000805000

77 JIMMY SMITH PEDALS

I saw Jimmy Smith only once, but when I did, I was focusing intensely on his pedal work. When playing a swinging tune, he would tap on the B in the middle of the pedal staff and occasionally play a black key above or below the B, then come back to thumping on the B. The brief thumps on the other keys gave the bass line a slightly different color and really let me hear the pedals. Try it yourself.

78 MELODY WITH LEFT HAND

This is another Jimmy Smith trick. When playing a ballad, Smith would play chords in the right hand and outline the melody with the left hand on the lower manual. The first few drawbars were pushed in to make the range comfortable. The bass was played in the pedals, with the roots and 5ths on beats 1 and 3.

79 — MELODIC MINOR HARMONY

It's a little hard to figure out the math of the altered scale, so I cheat. If you play a melodic minor scale a half step above the root of an alt7th chord, you get the altered scale. For example, over B7alt, go up a half step and use the C melodic minor scale for improvising.

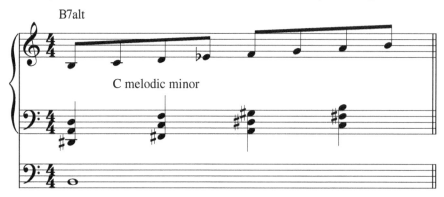

80 — LOCRIAN AND SUPER LOCRIAN HARMONY

A similar trick can be used with Locrian and Super Locrian modes. These scales work great over m7♭5 chords. The Super Locrian has a ♮9th which has a very distinctive sound. In bar 1, we play a major scale a half step above the B root to get a perfect scale for soloing Bm7♭5 chords. In bar 2, a melodic minor scale starting a minor 3rd over the root gives us that great ♮9th sound. Think, "Over m7♭5 chords with a ♮9th sound, play a melodic minor scale a minor 3rd above the root." Got that? Good!

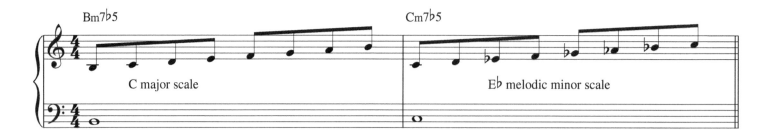

81 BIG HAMMOND VOICINGS

Right-hand organ voicings are usually made of a pianistic shell in the lowest three notes, then usually another note on top. Because organists often have to comp with one hand, the voicings tend to be bigger. Our left hand and foot plug along in an F blues while the right hand makes stabs with the half-fat setting and fast Leslie. The chord in bar 1 is, from the bottom up, ♭7th-3rd-13th-tonic. Notice how few notes have to move to get to the IV chord in bar 2. The last bar has a great-sounding II-V that moves just one note. Transpose these voicings to 12 keys to have the ultimate Hammond chords for the blues.

🔊 TIP 81

Upper Manual: 888000888   C3/Leslie fast
Lower Manual: 838000000   Pedals: 70

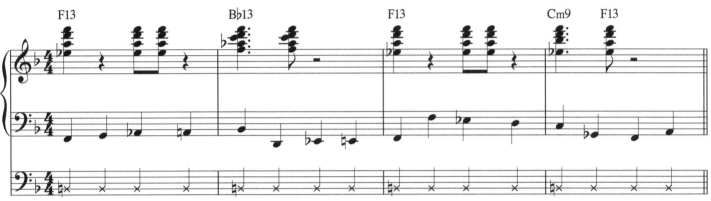

82 AUGMENTED SCALE

This is a modern symmetrical scale that can be used with great effect once in a while. Want to be a hip jazz guy? The next time you come to a C (or any other) major 7th chord, play Cmaj7♯5 and the C augmented scale (C-D♯-E-G-G♯-B-C) instead. This harmony is kind of what maj7♯11 harmony was in the 1960s. All the kids were doin' it. And you know how we roll; let's find another cool application. How about a C augmented scale over Am(maj7)? You get a cool sound with a few ethnic-sounding notes.

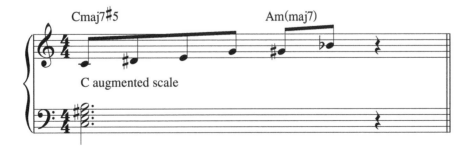

 83 B MAJOR AUGMENTED SCALE OVER "GIANT STEPS"

If you are a jazz guy, you know that "Giant Steps" is the holy grail of tunes. If you can blow on this one, people will think you are cool. Next time you are on your third chorus of this Coltrane classic and have no idea what to play, try the B augmented scale (B-D-D♯-F♯-G-A♯) over the whole progression. Watch the expression of your bandmates when you do this.

 85 NICOLAS SLONIMSKY

While we're talking about Coltrane, let's talk about what he practiced. Many of Coltrane's harmonic ideas – as well as the bridge chords of "Giant Steps" – come from Nicolas Slonimsky's *Thesaurus of Scales and Melodic Patterns*. (It's rumored that Arnold Schoenberg was also a fan.) If you are an improviser, scales are your weapon. The more you know (in all 12 keys), the more sounds you can get and the more directions you can go in. This freedom is what creates great solos and an individual sound.

 85 McCOY PIANO VOICINGS

These forms come from piano but you can use them on organ to get a real stacked-4th sound if you are playing with a bassist or pedaling a low C. These cool chords work over lots of other chords, too. You get four permutations for each key. If you transpose these chords to 12 keys, you have a whole two-handed system of comping over almost every chord change.

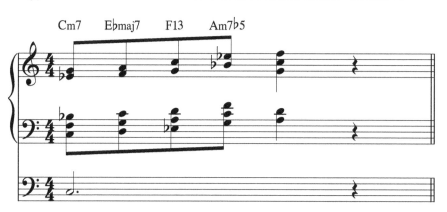

Upper Manual: 008080000   Vibrato/Percussion/Leslie to taste   Pedals: 70

86 A FORM AND B FORM

While we're at it, dig these voicings. These are most associated with pianist Bill Evans. The first two bars of this exercise are the first thing most beginning jazz piano students learn in 12 keys. That's what you should do, too. These is no better way to learn chord tones and the "grid" of the different keys. Bar 3 shows these chords in what we call Drop-2 voicing; in other words, the second note from the top is placed at the bottom of the voicing. Bar 4 has the chords in Drop 3. Try doing this for all your one-handed voices. This spacing is great when writing for a horn section as well.

Upper Manual: 008080000   Vibrato/Percussion/Leslie to taste
Lower Manual: 808000000

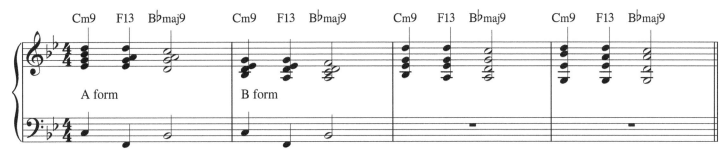

87 DRAWBAR FOLDBACK

What in the world is drawbar foldback? It's an electrical principle inside the Hammond. The 1' drawbar doesn't play pitches above F#4. At G4 the pitch drops an octave. Also, at the 16' drawbar, the reverse is true. You will notice that the lowest and second lowest octave on the Hammond sound the same.

88 MESSIAEN MODE 3 FOR SEAN WAYLAND

Olivier Messiaen (1908–1992) was a 20th century French composer who wrote lots of unusual-sounding organ music. His music utilized symmetrical scales he called Modes of Limited Transposition. The scales can be transposed only a certain number of times, hence the name. The first mode is the whole-tone scale (C-D-E-F#-G#-A#-C). The second mode is the diminished scale (C-Db-Eb-E-Gb-G-A-Bb-C). The third mode is the focus of this example. This scale sounds pretty different from our Bach scales. Try transposing it into 12 keys, using it over everything. It has major 3rds and minor 3rds, so it has qualities of both. Notice how the pattern of 1-2-b3-3 repeats on every major 3rd (there's the symmetry). For this device, the jazz pianist Sean Wayland is a great artist to listen to. He also has many great exercises on his website. Do an Internet search for him!

89 MESSIAEN MODE 7

This is the other big mode from Messiaen. They say all the other Modes of Limited Transposition are truncations of 3 and 7, so these are the only two I memorize. Then I just leave a few notes out to get the other modes. Messiaen himself has a text that explains his system, *La technique de mon language musical* ("The Technique of My Musical Language"). Mode 7 is actually a chromatic scale with two notes missing, the major 3rd and the dominant 7th. Try using this over Cmaj7 chords.

90 SIT UP STRAIGHT

The organ is a difficult instrument to play, physically. Good posture will really fight fatigue and enable you to play the pedals all night without getting tired. Also, in the words of a familiar phrase: "Don't forget to breathe."

91 WORK OUT

This is an extension of the last tip. Get some sort of exercise routine in your life. I have come to believe that playing music is mainly physical process. Having your body in top form will make you relaxed and strengthen your muscle memory which, to me, is the real thing that makes you good at music. What's the book where the guy says you have to do something for 10,000 hours to be a master? (Oh, yeah, Malcolm Gladwell's *Outliers: The Story of Success*.) Anyway, here's the point: When you see people playing music great and are marveled by their abilities, realize that they put the time in and it feels easy for them.

92 SOUND DIFFERENT

Develop your own sound on your instrument. Want a big way to do that? In the words of Miles Davis, "Take the horn out yo' mouth." Play less than other people. Most people are just running a bunch of crap because they are scared. Construct phrases with space, tell a story, and listen.

93 MUSIC IS THE EASY PART

In my travels, I've come to believe that playing the instrument is the easy part of being a musician. One has to navigate social media and deal with publicists, agents, cut throats, and backstabbers… The music business is tough, so get ready to grow thick skin. There will be lots of rejection on your way to the top. Try to take it in stride. Slow and steady does win the race.

94 DON'T CANCEL GIGS

Don't sub out a gig you've committed to if something slightly better comes along. In the long run, people will stop calling you if they think you are unreliable. There are exceptions, but in general the key to being a good sideman is being someone who can be trusted to be there and be a part of the team.

95 DON'T TRANSCRIBE

When I was a kid in school, the big contest was "Who Transcribes More Solos?" People walked around with books of transcriptions. Here's the thing about transcribing: You end up sounding like someone else. To sound like you, come up with your own approach. I think it's important to do few transcriptions, and I highly recommend learning some selections from the *Charlie Parker Omnibook*. I believe this is the most important text for learning how to improvise.

96 DON'T PRACTICE

Okay, here's where I start to talk really crazy. In the beginning it's important to practice, but when I hear people who have been playing for many years say, "I practice four hours a day," I feel like they are trying too hard. I think practicing is important for classical music, but if you are a person doing gigs, it's a little unnecessary. In general, trying too hard in music pushes it away from you. The more you relax, the more you will get the real spirit.

97 MAINTAIN PERSPECTIVE

Don't place too much emphasis on any achievement, concert, album, solo, etc. Musicians have huge egos and don't see that there are a lot of talented people. It's not so super important when you play a burning F blues solo.

98 PLOUGH DILIGENTLY

There is a Taoist mantra that works well for trying to achieve difficult things like being a rock star: "Plough diligently and expect no harvest."

99 GET SOCIAL

Facebook, YouTube, and Twitter are the new tools artists have to spread the word. Become skilled in using these platforms and watch your fan base grow.

100 HAVE FUN

If you are not having a good time with a certain band or style of music, quit. The whole point of playing music is to feel great and have fun.

101 MAKE FRIENDS

Be supportive to your bandmates, both musically and personally. Playing music with another person is an intimate event. Enjoy and nurture the connections you make with the people you play music with. A group of like-minded individuals who love and respect each other can achieve miracles.